To Robert and Norah Nichols

E. J. MOERAN

Songs of Springtime

Seven Elizabethan poems set for unaccompanied SATB chorus

NOVELLO
part of **WiseMusic**Group

EXCLUSIVELY DISTRIBUTED BY
HAL•LEONARD®

CONTENTS

NOTE—When the work is performed as a whole, the sequence herein must be followed.

SONGS OF SPRINGTIME

Seven Elizabethan Poems set to music for Mixed Chorus (S.A.T.B.)

BY

E. J. MOERAN

Nº 1. Under the Greenwood Tree

SHAKESPEARE

NOVELLO AND COMPANY

Who doth am - bi - tion shun And loves to live i' the

Who doth am - bi - tion shun_ And loves_ to live i' the

Who doth am - bi - tion shun And loves_ to live i' the

Who doth am - bi - tion shun And loves to live i' the

sun, Seek - ing the food he eats And pleased with what he

sun,_ Seek - ing the food_ he eats And pleased with what_ he

sun, Seek - ing the food he eats And pleased with what he

sun, Seek - ing the food_ he eats And pleased with what he

gets, Come hi - ther, come hi - ther, come hi - ther:

gets, Come hi - ther, come hi - ther, come hi - ther:

gets,_ Come hi - ther, come hi - ther, come hi - ther:

gets, Come hi - ther, come hi - ther, come hi - ther:

SONGS OF SPRINGTIME

Seven Elizabethan Poems set to music for Mixed Chorus (S. A. T. B.)

BY

E. J. MOERAN

Nº 2. The River-God's Song

JOHN FLETCHER (1579-1625)

SONGS OF SPRINGTIME

Seven Elizabethan Poems set to music for Mixed Chorus (S.A.T.B.)

BY

E. J. MOERAN

Nº 3. Spring, the Sweet Spring

THOMAS NASHE (1567–1601)

f mf mp f
sing, Cuck - oo, jug - jug, pu - we, to-wit-ta - woo! The palm and
sing, Cuck - oo, jug - jug, pu - we, to-wit-ta - woo! The palm and
sing, Cuck - oo, jug - jug, pu - we, to-wit-ta - woo! The palm and
sing, Cuck - oo, jug - jug, pu - we, to-wit-ta - woo! The palm and
mp mf
may make coun-try hou-ses gay, Lambs frisk and play, the shep-herds pipe all
may make coun-try hou-ses gay, Lambs frisk and play, the shep-herds pipe all
may make coun-try hou-ses gay, Lambs frisk and play, the shep-herds pipe all
may make coun-try hou-ses gay, Lambs frisk and play, the shep-herds pipe all
p cresc. f mp
day, And we hear aye birds tune this mer-ry lay, Cuck - oo, jug -
day, And we hear aye birds tune this mer-ry lay, Cuck - oo, jug -
day, And we hear aye birds tune this mer-ry lay, Cuck - oo, jug -
day, And we hear aye birds tune this mer - ry lay, Cuck - oo, jug -

f
decresc.
-oo, Cuck-oo, Cuck-oo, Cuck-oo, Cuck-oo, jug-jug, pu-
jug-jug, pu-we, to-wit-ta-woo, to-wit-ta-woo! Cuck-oo, pu-
jug-jug, pu-we, to-wit-ta-woo, pu-we, to-wit-ta-woo! pu-
jug-jug, pu-we, to-wit-ta-
pp
-we, to-wit-ta-woo! to-wit-ta-woo!
-we, to-wit-ta-woo! (lips closed)
-we, to-wit-ta-woo! to-wit-ta-woo! to-wit-ta-woo!
-woo! to-wit-ta-woo! (lips closed)
ppp
mf
molto allargando
ff
(lips closed)
Spring, the sweet Spring, the sweet Spring!
Spring, the sweet Spring, the sweet Spring!
Spring, the sweet Spring, the sweet Spring, the sweet Spring!
Spring, the sweet Spring, the sweet Spring, the sweet Spring!

SONGS OF SPRINGTIME

Seven Elizabethan Poems set to music for Mixed Chorus (S.A.T.B.)

BY

E. J. MOERAN

№ 4. Love is a Sickness

SAMUEL DANIEL (1562-1619)

14

SONGS OF SPRINGTIME

Seven Elizabethan Poems set to music for Mixed Chorus (S.A.T.B.)

BY

E. J. MOERAN

Nº 5. Sigh no more, Ladies

SHAKESPEARE

never: Then sigh not so,— but let them go, And be you blithe and bon-ny, Con-

never: Then sigh not so, but let them go, And be you blithe and bon-ny, Con-

never: Then sigh not so, but let them go, And be you blithe and bon-ny, Con-

never: Then sigh not so, but let them go, And be you blithe and bon-ny, Con-

poco accel.   poco animato
-vert-ing all—your sounds of woe In-to Hey non-ny, Hey non-ny, Hey non-ny,

-vert-ing all—your sounds of woe In-to Hey non-ny, Hey non-ny, Hey non-ny,

-vert-ing all—your sounds of woe In-to Hey non-ny, Hey non-ny, Hey non-ny,

-vert-ing all—your sounds of woe In-to Hey non-ny, Hey non-ny, Hey non-ny,
poco accel.   poco animato

Hey non-ny, non-ny, non-ny non-ny non-ny,

Hey non-ny, non-ny, non-ny non-ny non-ny,

Hey non-ny, Hey non-ny, Hey non-ny non-ny,

Hey non-ny, Hey, Hey non-ny, Hey non-ny,

18

SONGS OF SPRINGTIME

Seven Elizabethan Poems set to music for Mixed Chorus (S.A.T.B.)

BY

E. J. MOERAN

Nº 6. Good Wine

WILLIAM BROWNE (1591–1643)

nev - er shall do mine; I have no cra-dle go - ing yet, Not I, by this good

nev - er shall do mine; I have no cra-dle go - ing yet, Not I, by this good

nev - er shall do mine; I have no cra-dle go - ing yet, Not I, by this good

nev - er shall do mine; I have no cra-dle go - ing yet, Not I, by this good

wine.

wine.

wine. No wife at home to

wine. No wife at home to send for me, No hogs are

La la la la la la la la la, La la la la la la

La la la la la la la la la, La la la la la la

send for me, No hogs are in my ground, No suit in law to

in my ground, No suit in law to

ff p subito
cresc.
drink of the sher - ry, That makes us so
drink of the sher - ry, That makes us so
drink of the sher - ry, That makes us so mer - ry, To drink of the sher - ry, That
drink of the sher - ry, That makes us so mer - ry, To drink of the sher - ry, That
fff
mer - ry, To drink of the sher - ry, That makes us so mer - ry, To drink
makes us so mer - ry, To drink of the sher - ry, That makes us so mer - ry, To drink
rall.
allargando
— of the sher - ry, That makes us so mer - ry, And plump as the lus - ty grape.

SONGS OF SPRINGTIME

Seven Elizabethan Poems set to music for Mixed Chorus (S.A.T.B.)

BY

E. J. MOERAN

Nº 7. To Daffodils

HERRICK